To Mom and Dad, for teaching me to care for our precious planet.
To Rescate Wildlife Rescue Center, for saving Grecia.—B. M.

To all those amazing and kind humans that have always
encouraged me to keep creating. Thank you.—D. H.

Text copyright © 2024 Becca McMurdie
Illustrations copyright © 2024 Diana Hernández

First published in 2024 by Page Street Kids
an imprint of
Page Street Publishing Co.
27 Congress Street, Suite 1511
Salem, MA 01970
www.pagestreetpublishing.com

Distributed by Macmillan, sales in Canada by The Canadian Manda Group

24 25 26 27 28 CCO 5 4 3 2 1
ISBN-13: 978-1-64567-868-7
ISBN-10: 1-64567-868-7

CIP data for this book is available from the Library of Congress.

This book was typeset in Alegreya Sans.
The illustrations were done digitally.
Cover and book design by Katie Beasley for Page Street Kids
Edited by Kayla Tostevin for Page Street Kids

Printed and bound in Shenzhen, Guangdong, China

Page Street Publishing uses only materials from suppliers who are committed to
responsible and sustainable forest management.

Page Street Publishing protects our planet by donating to nonprofits like The Trustees,
which focuses on local land conservation.

BUILDING A BEAK

How a Toucan's Rescue Inspired the World

written by **Becca McMurdie**
illustrated by **Diana Hernández**

PAGE
STREET
KiDS

High in the Costa Rican treetops, a toucan named
Grecia soared from branch to branch,

picked berries,

preened her feathers,

and sang for all the creatures
of the rainforest.

Each night, she curled her red and yellow beak next to her wing and slept in her favorite avocado tree.

One evening, voices and footsteps approached.
Yells and taunts echoed through the trees.

Sticks and rocks flew, until . . .

Grecia fell from the branches. She could
not move. She could not sing.

All night, she lay on the dark forest floor,
far from her favorite avocado tree.

The next morning, human voices neared again.

Gentle hands carried her.

A veterinarian examined Grecia's beak. Grecia trembled and squawked but was too weak to fly away.

The vet shook her head. "She might not survive," she said.
"Without a beak, a toucan cannot sing, eat, bathe, or balance."

"Then she needs a new beak," said the vet's assistant.

Soon, the news spread.

Many offered to help. Dentists. Engineers. Bird experts.

For Grecia

Someone brought a toucan beak
from a museum.

Got well soon!
Grecia

Children brought cards and made beaks out of Styrofoam.

Nothing worked. And people had questions.

"Who did this?"

"Why would anyone hurt a toucan?"

"How could this happen?"

Grecia hid behind a tree branch in her
new habitat, keeping her distance.

As days passed, Grecia got stronger.

She could not pluck fruit from branches, but she learned how to scoop food with her bottom beak, like a pelican. It was hard work, but she stayed focused.

"This bird wants to live," the vet said.
"We can't give up on her."

When it seemed they had tried everything, the phone rang. An engineer had a 3D printer used to make nose cones for airplanes.

He thought he could use the printer
to make a beak for Grecia.

Printing a beak for
a toucan had never
been done before.

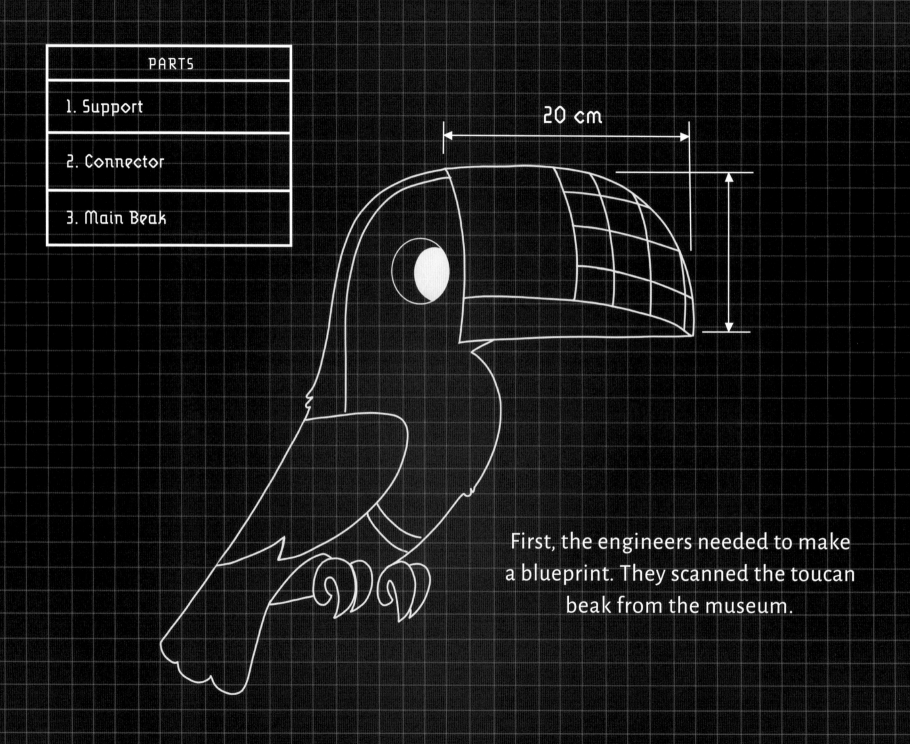

PARTS

1. Support

2. Connector

3. Main Beak

20 cm

First, the engineers needed to make a blueprint. They scanned the toucan beak from the museum.

To design the new beak to be just the right size, the engineers needed to take measurements of Grecia's face with a scanner.

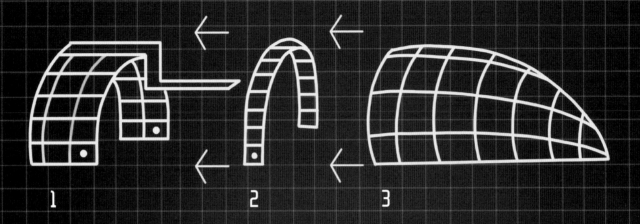

1   2   3

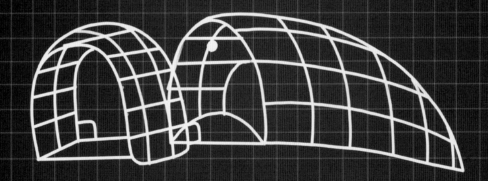

They would have to hold a machine close to her, and she would have to stay still for a long time. But toucans don't like to stay still.

The rescue team covered Grecia's eyes with a towel and held her while the engineers scanned. Grecia did not move.

"I think she knows we're helping her," the vet said,
with tears in her eyes.

With the scans, the engineers adjusted their blueprint. Then,
they printed the new upper beak. It looked like a regular beak.
It was the perfect size.

But would it work?

Outside the rescue center, people helped
Grecia a different way.

Students started a petition.

Grown-ups and children marched, chanted, and sang.

They sang for Grecia, and for all the creatures of the rainforest, since she could not sing for them herself.

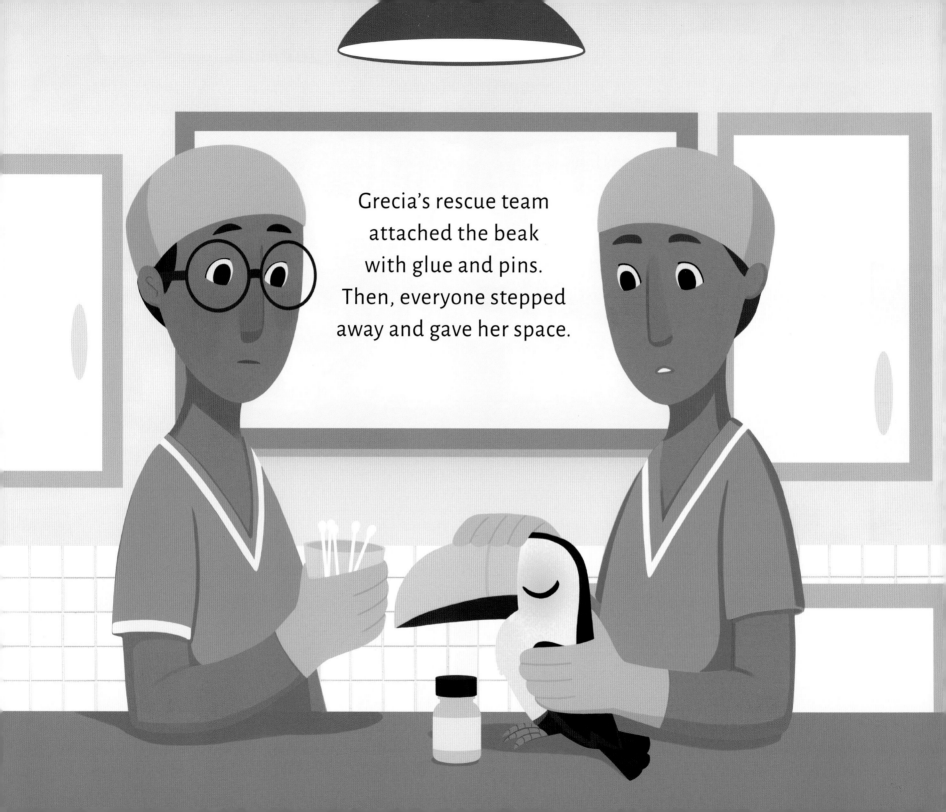

Grecia's rescue team
attached the beak
with glue and pins.
Then, everyone stepped
away and gave her space.

Grecia tilted up and down, feeling her new face.
Someone placed a grape next to her.

She stared at it, as if wondering, *Can I do it?*

Then Grecia opened wide, plucked the grape, and swallowed.

Everyone cried and cheered.

For the first time since her injury, Grecia sang.

Perhaps this was her way of saying,
Thank you, thank you, thank you.

And, thanks to Grecia, the Costa Rican president passed a new law the following year, making it illegal to harm wildlife.

Grecia didn't know she'd inspired such important change.
She stayed focused on her favorite activities,
plucking and peeling fruit.

The rescue team decided not to let Grecia back into the wild. Her new beak needed routine checkups and adjustments.

Instead, they built her a big habitat, with lots of trees and branches, so she could live as comfortably as possible.

They even gave her a mate, so she could have a family.

Grecia never flew in the rainforest again.
But she could still perch on branches, pick berries,
bathe, preen her feathers, and of course, sing.

And around the world, people continue to sing for her, and for all the creatures of the rainforest.

AUTHOR'S NOTE

Grecia's experience shows us that all beings, no matter how small, can leave a big impact on our planet. Her story also reminds us that while humans can cause harm and destruction, we are even more capable of collaboration, compassion, and love. At the time of Grecia's injury, there were no local laws to punish people who abused animals. Her story fueled an animal welfare movement to change that. Grecia is now an international symbol for the wildlife protection movement.

By reading animal rescue stories like Grecia's and discussing them with friends and family, you, too, are helping to build awareness about the importance of protecting our rainforests. To learn more about the incredible team that cared for Grecia and rescues hundreds of other animals each year, visit the Rescate Wildlife Rescue Center at www.rescatewildlife.org.

TOUCAN TIMELINE

January 2015: Local farmers in Grecia, Costa Rica, find an injured chestnut-mandibled toucan with a missing upper beak. Grecia the toucan is brought to the Rescate Wildlife Rescue Center, formerly known as Zooave, in Alajuela, Costa Rica.

January 2016: Veterinarians successfully attach Grecia's prosthetic beak.

December 2021: Grecia dies peacefully of natural causes.

February 2015: In response to extensive social and news media coverage of Grecia's injury, an international team of dentists, veterinarians, and engineers from several 3D printing companies join forces to begin designing a prosthetic beak for her.

June 2017: Costa Rica passes an anti-animal-cruelty law, criminalizing the intentional killing or harming of pets and wildlife.

THE BEAK AND BEYOND

- Grecia's true gender is unknown. The only way to find out would have been a blood test, but caretakers thought the test would cause her too much stress. We refer to Grecia as "she" in this text as when researching this story that is the pronoun Rescate's rescue team used in interviews.

- The rescue center decided not to paint Grecia's new beak after attaching it. They thought it was important to leave it white, as a reminder to visitors of the suffering she endured.

- Grecia never socialized much with the toucan the rescue team gave her as a mate. During her time in the sanctuary, Grecia sang daily and attracted another wild toucan, who regularly perched outside her enclosure and sang along with her.

BIBLIOGRAPHY

Arias, L. "Grecia: The Costa Rican Toucan with the prosthetic beak." *The Tico Times.* 11 August 2016. https://ticotimes.net/2016/08/11/grecia-toucan-new-cage.

Conn, Clayton. "Grecia: the toucan with a prosthetic beak." *Outlook BBC.* 17 December 2019. https://www.bbc.co.uk/programmes/p07y6023?fbclid=IwAR1f6TyGZVLYmDaA2gOBu3Fd7TTu-o78IdP7QYtisrfmAjvEogJDJeOFXK8.

Heredia, Paula. "Toucan Nation." Animal Planet. 11 June 2016.

Kahn, Carrie. "After Losing Half a Beak, Grecia the Toucan Becomes a Symbol Against Abuse." *Weekend Edition Saturday.* NPR. 27 August 2016, https://www.npr.org/sections/parallels/2016/08/27/491372643/after-losing-half-a-beak-grecia-the-toucan-becomes-a-symbol-against-abuse.

Koslow, Tyler. "3D Systems Details Process Behind 3D Printed Prosthetic Beak for Grecia the Toucan." 3DPrint.com Website. 22 August 2016. https://3dprint.com/146721/grecia-the-toucan-3d-systems/.

McMurdie, Rebecca. "Interview with Jeanne Marie Pittman." 8 January 2022.

"Nicuesa Lodge in the news: Helping save Grecia the toucan in Costa Rica." *Playa Nicuesa Rainforest Lodge* (blog). July 2016. https://www.nicuesalodge.com/blog/nicuesa-lodge-in-the-newshelping-save-grecia-the-toucan-in-costa-rica.

Pittman, Jeanne Marie. E-mail to Rebecca McMurdie. 25 February 2022.

Quesada Quiros, Magali. Email to Rebecca McMurdie. 24 December 2021.

Simon, Scott. "Thanks To Technology, Toucan Gets a Second Beak on Life." *Weekend Edition Saturday.* NPR. 14 February 2015. https://www.npr.org/2015/02/14/386227452/thanks-to-technology-toucan-gets-a-second-beak-on-life.